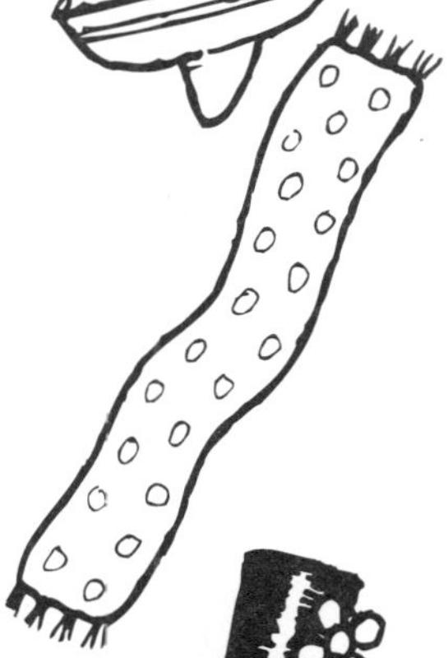

Contents

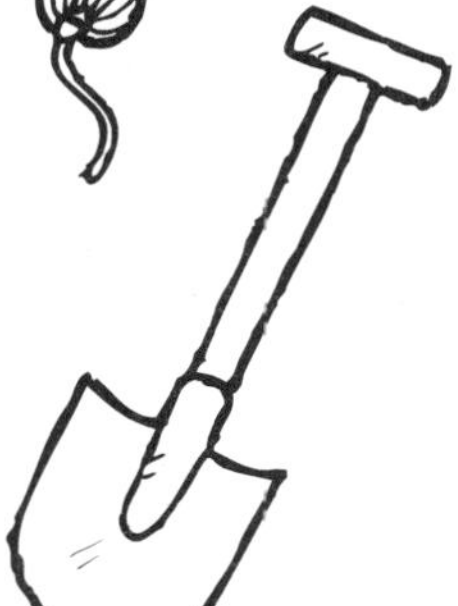

Introduction

Speech has a range of purposes. Socially, it enables children to communicate. It empowers them to initiate and respond to conversations with adults or other children, and to express themselves within a group. It frees children from the present and enables them to talk about past experiences and events, and helps them to discuss probabilities as well as the future.

However, children need something to talk about, and therefore experiences should stimulate them to ask questions *and* listen to answers. From early baby talk, children use and extend their vocabulary to develop and widen their understanding of the world around them. Perceptive and supportive adults ask questions that are open-ended, requiring children to express their ideas fully, rather than answering in monosyllables.

Speaking and listening are both active processes, and require interaction between people. Adults, therefore, need to give time to listening to what children say. A reluctant talker or a reluctant listener may not fully understand the conversation; in such a case, adults need to think about the way in which they themselves are expressing something. Children often model their speech on that of adults, therefore as adults we have a responsibility to listen, adapt and respond in a way that is meaningful to each individual child.

As speech shapes the child intellectually and socially, so too it encourages their imagination. A fascinating world of fiction is opened up to children through listening to stories and poems, which encourages them to role-play, 'make believe' and create stories of their own.

This book suggests activities that help to develop the wide range of skills used in speaking and listening. The ideas are structured developmentally towards aims related to the Early Learning Goals and Baseline Assessment Scales for this area of learning.

Early Learning Goals

The Early Learning Goals are the six areas of learning that provide young children with a foundation for later achievement when entering compulsory education. Speaking and listening are a prerequisite for all areas of the curriculum, but form an essential part of the Early Learning Goals for Language and literacy. Children's progress may be at different rates – some may need opportunities to extend their skills, while others may require extra reinforcement. The activities in this book, therefore, offer ways to support younger children, or those who require a different rate of progression, and also suggest extension ideas for older or more able children.

Baseline Assessment

Baseline Assessment of all children aged four to five years old on entry into primary school, is a legal requirement. This includes speaking and listening as one of the basic skills. The information obtained from these assessments helps teachers to plan their teaching to suit the needs of individual children, and to measure their future progress.

Skills development chart

The Skills development chart on page 32 shows how this book has taken the aims of the Early Learning Goals for speaking and listening, and linked them to the measurements of the Baseline Assessment Scales, to form a developmental structure leading to a 'merged' final achievement.

Each activity's learning outcome provides the 'I can...' achievement on the chart, while the smaller leaves at the top of the chart represent one of four main kinds of speaking and listening: Experiential/social; Logical; Imaginative and Listening. Although Listening has only two activities listed, it is of course paramount to all the other activities.

Different kinds of speaking and listening

- **Experiential/social** – this involves children in talking about their own experiences, thoughts and feelings. It develops the social skills required to initiate and respond in conversations and discussions.
- **Logical** – talk is a vital instrument for learning. It helps children to question, evaluate, make sense of events and information, and develop their understanding of new concepts.
- **Imaginative** – listening to stories, poems and rhymes introduces children to the richness and variety of language, developing their vocabulary and enabling them to talk about and initiate imaginative and new ideas of their own.
- **Listening** – this is essential to the development of all kinds of talk.

How to use this book

Each activity in this book provides a practical group activity, which is supported with a photocopiable sheet on the opposite page. This photocopiable activity further develops and reinforces the learning aim. It can also be used as an assessment record for each child.

If the sheet is intended to be used by individual children, and can be kept as a record, it is referred to as an 'Individual recording'; if it is intended to be used by a group of children together, or does not form a written record, then it is referred to as an 'Individual task'.

Where the photocopiable activities involve the children in cutting and gluing the various elements of the sheet, it is suggested that you make a second copy on which to record your observations.

Progression

The order of the activities in this book progresses laterally through each of the different kinds of speaking and listening, starting at the bottom of the Skills development chart, and moving across at each level, and upwards towards the final aims at the top.

Home links

Speaking and listening are essentially linked to the interactions in speech that occur at home in everyday situations, so it is vitally important that the child's family is involved wherever possible. The Home links section therefore suggests ways in which parents can become involved in and support their children's learning.

All about me

Learning objective
To talk about themselves.

Group size
Up to five children.

What you need
The photocopiable sheet; a personal item belonging to each child (hat, glove, shoe, toy, ribbon and so on); a personal item belonging to yourself.

Preparation
Copy the photocopiable sheet so that you have one for each child and one for yourself. Fill in the first two boxes of your copy of the sheet.

What to do
Start by holding up the item belonging to yourself. Explain to the children that it is yours, then tell them something about it (what you use it for, its colour, when you got it and so on).

Show the children the selection of their personal items and ask if anyone would like to talk about the one that belongs to them. Encourage the children to talk about their items in the same way. Reluctant children may prefer to talk to an adult on their own later. Alternatively, if you start describing their item, they may then join in.

Hold up your copy of the photocopiable sheet and invite the children to talk about the pictures. Look at the picture of a baby, and talk to them about when you were a baby, then a toddler, and the different things you did at those times. Finish by saying, 'Now I am grown up, and yesterday I...', then talk about something you do as an adult.

Individual recording
Give each child a copy of the photocopiable sheet. Talk to them about when they were babies. Can they remember anything they have been told about when they were very small? Ask open-ended questions, for example 'Where were you born?'. Give them time to think about their answer (such as in hospital, at home). Then talk about when they were toddlers, and ask them about that time. Do they remember learning to talk? Did they say anything funny? Finally, encourage the children to think of something they did yesterday. Scribe a simple sentence for them in each of the blank sections, and let them colour in the pictures.

Support
If children are unable to talk about themselves when they were younger, encourage them to talk about other babies or toddlers they know. Ask, 'Do you think you ever did anything like that? What else do you think you might have done?'.

Extension
Can the children think of more than one thing that they have done recently? Record how many ideas they talk about.

Assessment
If a child appears reluctant to talk, check whether they fully understand the questions. Can the children talk confidently to each other about themselves?

Home links
A few days before the activity, ask parents to talk about their children's early days with them.

All about me

When I was a baby

I ________________

____

____

When I was a toddler

I ________________

____

____

Now I am ________

Yesterday I ________

____

____

What's the difference?

Learning objective
To develop the vocabulary to talk about differences.

Group size
Up to five children.

What you need
The photocopiable sheet; collections of items that are similar but different (such as plain, striped or patterned scarves, or different types of shoes).

Preparation
Copy the photocopiable sheet so that you have one for each child and one for yourself.

What to do
Start by showing the group one of the collections. Invite the children to talk about how the items are different from each other. Encourage them to look at patterns, material, shape, size and colour. Develop this further by discussing *how* the patterns are different, what the various materials *feel* like and so on. Help the children to find the right vocabulary to describe the differences (longer/shorter, soft/rough). Then remind them that in some ways the items are also the same – they are *all* scarves, they can all be worn and so on. Can they think of other ways the items are the same? Repeat the process with the other collections.

Individual task
Give each child a copy of the photocopiable sheet and talk about the pictures. Establish that both pictures are of clowns but they are not quite the same. Now ask them to discuss how the two pictures differ. Can they do more than notice *what* is different by talking about *how* it is different? For example, the clowns' trousers are different because one pair is striped and the other is spotted. Assess how many details each child sees, and note in particular how limited or extensive their relevant vocabulary is.

Support
Some children may not see all the differences, but allow them to express themselves as fully as they can about the things that they do notice. Then mention one or two other differences. What can they say about them?

Extension
Encourage the children to draw other things in each picture which are different. For example, they might draw the same circus tent in each picture, but in different positions.

Assessment
Did the children understand what was required of them? Were they able to discriminate between the pictures? If not, check their perceptual skills through other discrimination games such as puzzles or snap cards. If the children were able to point to the differences but were unable to explain what they perceived, consider how well they verbalize differences in their everyday experiences. For example, can they discuss how one toy (child, game, piece of fruit) differs from another?

Home links
Ask parents to draw attention to differences around the home, for example sizes of cups or patterns on jumpers.

What's the difference?

Goldilocks

Learning objective
To listen to a story and retell it.

Group size
Up to five children.

What you need
The photocopiable sheet; a picture book of the story of 'Goldilocks and the Three Bears'.

Preparation
Copy the photocopiable sheet so that you have one for each child and one for yourself.

What to do
Gather the children together and read the story to them. Observe whether they listen attentively or are easily distracted. Afterwards, ask them which part of the story they liked best. Can they tell you why they liked that part? Briefly recap on the story together, encouraging the children to think it through by asking questions such as, 'And then what happened?' or 'Can you remember what Goldilocks did then?' and so on.

Show the children your copy of the photocopiable sheet, and draw attention to the pictures. Explain that they show the story of 'Goldilocks and the Three Bears'. Let them talk about the pictures in general terms. Encourage them to point out things by saying 'What can you see in this picture?' and so on.

Individual recording
Give each child a copy of the photocopiable sheet. Ask them whether they can see from the pictures where the story begins. Then ask the children to tell you *how* the story began. Can they remember what happened? Move through the pictures, allowing the children time to look at them in detail, before they go on to retell the story using the pictures as prompts. Reluctant children may be helped by asking them, 'What part of the story does this picture remind you of?'. Make brief assessment notes on each child's sheet.

Support
Make sure younger children have plenty of opportunities to retell other short stories before using this activity. Help them with questions such as, 'The bears are going away from the cottage, but what is Goldilocks doing?' or 'What happened to the bowls of porridge?'.

Extension
Encourage the children to talk in as much detail as they can about the story. Some may be able to recall and identify differences between the pictures in the book and those on the photocopiable sheet.

Assessment
If a child is unable to tell the story, does this reflect on the way they appeared to listen to it? If they listened attentively, but could not retell the story, is it because their recall is poor, or did they have difficulty finding the right vocabulary?

Home links
Ask parents to involve their children in retelling stories from their books at home.

Goldilocks

When I went shopping

Learning objective
To talk about an event.

Group size
Up to ten children.

What you need
The photocopiable sheet.

Preparation
Copy the photocopiable sheet so that you have one for each child and one for yourself.

What to do
Start by talking to the children about something that you have done recently, for example going out to lunch with a friend. Give a few details, such as how you arranged to meet, where you went, what you had to eat and so on. Some children may be prompted to talk about a similar event of their own.

Now show the children the picture of the shopping precinct on the photocopiable sheet. Ask if they know what it is and talk in general terms about it, helping them with vocabulary, and encouraging them to identify details such as the type of shops and what you can buy there.

Individual recording
Give each child a copy of the photocopiable sheet, and ask them to tell you about a time when they visited the shops. Most children will remember such an occasion, but if they are reluctant to talk, encourage them by pointing to one of the shops, for example a shoe shop, and asking, 'Have you ever been to buy shoes?'. Help them to think about the event and tell you details such as who they went with and what they did afterwards. Make assessment notes on the back of each child's sheet.

Support
Some younger children may prefer to tell you about a different event, not related to the shop picture. If so, ask them to draw a picture of it on the back of the sheet and talk to you about it.

Extension
Record how many pieces of information the children gave about the event. Encourage them to describe what happened in the right order.

Assessment
Some young children may say, 'I can't remember' because they do not have the vocabulary to verbalize their thoughts. Observe them at other times and help them to talk about simple things that they have been doing.

Home links
Ask parents to recount events with their children, soon after they occur, and then to encourage the child to talk about the events to another adult.

When I went shopping

My day

Learning objective
To talk about events in sequence.

Group size
Up to five children.

What you need
The photocopiable sheet; a doll and its clothes; scissors; glue; A4 paper.

Preparation
Copy the photocopiable sheet so that you have two copies for each child and one for yourself.

What to do
Lay out all the doll's clothes and tell the children that you are going to dress the doll. Look at the clothes and ask, 'What comes first? What should the doll put on first of all?'. This is to ensure that the children are aware not only of the sequencing involved, but also of the vocabulary needed. Continue to dress the doll, encouraging the children to join in, stressing words and phrases such as: 'What comes next?' 'After that...' 'And then...' 'And last of all...'.

Individual recording
First, talk to the children about their day, using some of the terminology from the doll-dressing sequence. For example, 'What was the first thing you did when you got up this morning?'. Encourage them to think and talk about their day, making sure that the events are in the right order. Then show the children the photocopiable sheet, and talk about each picture. Lead them to realize that the pictures do not follow the right sequence. Show them how to cut up the pictures carefully and then discuss with them the correct order as they rearrange them and glue them onto the A4 sheets of paper. Make assessment notes for each child on their second copy of the sheet.

Support
Simplify the activity by reducing the number of cut-out pictures to four. Give any children who seemed confused plenty of other sequencing activities and spend time talking them through everyday events.

Extension
Ask children if they can tell you anything else that they do during the day. Can they show you where it would it fit in the order of pictures?

Assessment
Observe how well the children understand the idea of one thing following another, while dressing the doll. When discussing their own day, are they clear about the order of events or are their recollections disjointed?

Home links
Parents could help by involving children in the sequencing of simple household tasks such as baking a cake or sorting the washing. They could ask, 'What do we put in the cake next?' or 'Now what do we need to do?'.

My day

Listen and role-play

Learning objective
To listen to a taped story and role-play it.

Group size
Up to five children.

What you need
The photocopiable sheet; tape recorder; pencils; crayons; scissors.

Preparation
Record a short story, either familiar or made up, onto a tape recorder. Try to keep to two main characters, talking to each other in simple direct speech. Copy the photocopiable sheets so that you have two for each child and one for yourself. Cut out and illustrate the finger puppets on your photocopiable sheet to represent the two main characters in the story.

What to do
Show the children your two finger puppets and introduce them by name. Explain to the children that these two characters are in a story that they are going to listen to on the tape.

Play the tape and, as each character is mentioned, show the appropriate puppet by walking it across the table.

Individual task
Give each child a copy of the photocopiable sheet and help them to colour and cut out the characters. Encourage the children to talk about the story as they do so. Play the story again, showing the children how to walk the puppets across the table. When the story has finished, ask the children to retell the story in their own words, using the puppets to role-play the action. Record observations about each child on their second photocopiable sheet.

Support
Some children will be more confident if an adult takes the role of one puppet while they take the role of the other. Use this as an opportunity to move the story along by talking to the child through the puppet, helping them to develop their character's speaking part.

Extension
Make extra copies of the photocopiable sheet so that the children can role-play other stories or make up their own characters and story.

Assessment
How well did the children adapt to listening without visual clues or stimulation? How far were they able to remember the speaking parts of the characters in their role-plays? Did they re-enact the story without help from an adult? To encourage listening without visual clues, read other stories aloud without showing the children the pictures or set up an area where children can repeat the activity with taped stories.

Home links
Ask parents to make up their own stories at home, using some of the child's own toys to dramatize the action.

Listen and role-play

How does Teddy feel?

Learning objective
To talk about feelings.

Group size
Up to ten children for the story, then groups of five children for the activity.

What you need
The photocopiable sheet; a short story-book.

Preparation
Copy the photocopiable sheet for the children to have one each.

What to do
Read the children a short story, showing them the pictures, and drawing attention to any expressions shown on the faces of the characters that might indicate feelings.

In groups, encourage the children to talk about the characters in the story. Were they happy or sad? Were they lonely, angry, frightened or excited? Why did they feel like that? Did something happen, or not happen, to cause it?

Individual recording
Give each child a copy of the photocopiable sheet and ask them to look at the pictures of the teddy. Allow them time to study the pictures carefully. Tell them to look at the teddy in the first picture and ask, 'How is Teddy feeling?'. If they seem unable to answer, encourage them by asking if they think the teddy is enjoying himself. 'Did anyone in the story feel the same way?' 'Who?' 'Do they ever look like that?' 'When?'. Talk about each picture in the same way. Make brief assessment notes on the back of each child's sheet.

Support
Some young children can empathize very closely with the feelings of others, but are unable to explain it in words. Encourage them to alter their own facial expressions to match the picture. Limit the assessment to the first three pictures.

Extension
Can the children tell you about a time when they have felt happy? Has there been a time when they have felt angry or upset? What made them feel better again? Let them colour in the pictures of the teddy and then draw a picture of themselves on the back of the sheet, showing a time when they were happy or sad.

Assessment
How far were children able to identify and verbalize their feelings? If children can learn to express their feelings by talking about them, it can help to prevent temper tantrums and lead them to explain more clearly what they need. Try to develop this during other activities, and observe how much help children need on an individual basis.

Home links
Ask parents to talk about the feelings of characters in other story-books, encouraging associated vocabulary such as worried, shy, embarrassed, scared.

How does Teddy feel?

Teddy is feeling ____________

Teddy is feeling ____________

Teddy is feeling ____________

Teddy is feeling ____________

Teddy is feeling ____________

Teddy is feeling ____________

And then...

Learning objective
To predict and talk about what might happen next.

Group size
Up to five children.

What you need
The photocopiable sheet; a picture story-book which is new to the children.

Preparation
Copy the photocopiable sheet so that you have one for each child and one for yourself.

What to do
Start reading the story and talk about the first picture. Ask, 'And what do you think happened then?'. Accept and discuss briefly all the ideas that the children offer and the possible outcomes. Continue to read the story, and compare their predictions with what does actually happen. Stop the story from time to time where appropriate, including just before the ending, to ask the children to predict what will happen next. Observe which children are quick to offer ideas, and note whether others become more confident as the discussions are repeated.

Individual recording
Discuss each of the pictures on the photocopiable sheet in turn. Then, concentrate on the first picture and ask, 'If this was a story, what do you think would happen next?'. Notice whether the child offers one outcome or a sequence of outcomes. Suggestions might include: 'She will put the cake on the table', 'They will sing happy birthday' or 'The child will blow out the candles'. Others might even foresee a perfectly acceptable comic outcome, such as 'She will fall over and the cake will splosh on the floor!'. Essentially, the children should be encouraged to envisage any logical outcome. Continue with the other pictures, making notes on the back of each child's sheet.

Support
Offer the phrase 'I think that... will happen' to encourage the children. Help them to visualize the picture as a real-life situation. For example, 'Have you ever been to a birthday party? What happened?'.

Extension
Can the children suggest alternative outcomes for the last two pictures? For example in the third picture, the ball might go into the river and the puppy go in after it, or the puppy might reach the ball first.

Assessment
How well did the children understand the concept of projecting forwards? Were they able to visualize and talk about an outcome, or were they locked into the present situation offered in the picture?

Home links
Ask parents to pose questions which help children to think beyond an immediate situation. For example, 'What will happen if you go out in the rain without your coat on?'.

And then…

Once upon a time

Learning objective
To make up a story in role-play.

Group size
Up to four children.

What you need
The photocopiable sheet; a selection of dressing-up clothes; crayons; scissors; lolly sticks; glue.

Preparation
Copy the photocopiable sheet so that you have two for each child and one for yourself.

What to do
Allow the children to play freely with a selection of dressing-up clothes. Observe and listen to the variations of their play according to each child's viewpoint. After about ten minutes, if the children begin to play co-operatively, encourage them to develop a story between them by joining in for a while. If they are playing separately, record on each one's spare photocopiable sheet how far they are creating their own story. The story does not need to be original. Children may base their play on familiar characters or stories.

Individual task
Give each child a copy of the photocopiable sheet. Explain that they can make a mask to represent the character that they were playing in their story, or if they prefer, they can make up a new character. Help them to colour and cut out the mask and glue it onto the end of a lolly stick. Encourage them to talk about the story that they are going to use it for.

Afterwards, allow them time to role-play using their masks and the dressing-up clothes. Use this as an opportunity to make further observations.

Support
Make suggestions for a familiar character that they could base their mask on. Help them to develop a story by asking open-ended questions: 'What kind of rabbit (princess, fairy and so on) are you going to be?' 'What is going to happen in your story?'.

Extension
Some children may prefer to work as a pair or even a foursome, linking their characters to each other in a co-operative story.

Assessment
How far did the children develop a story beyond acting out their character? Did they imagine a scenario of what they did or what happened to them?

Home links
Ask parents to provide a dressing-up box at home, and encourage their children to retell the stories they have been playing.

Once upon a time

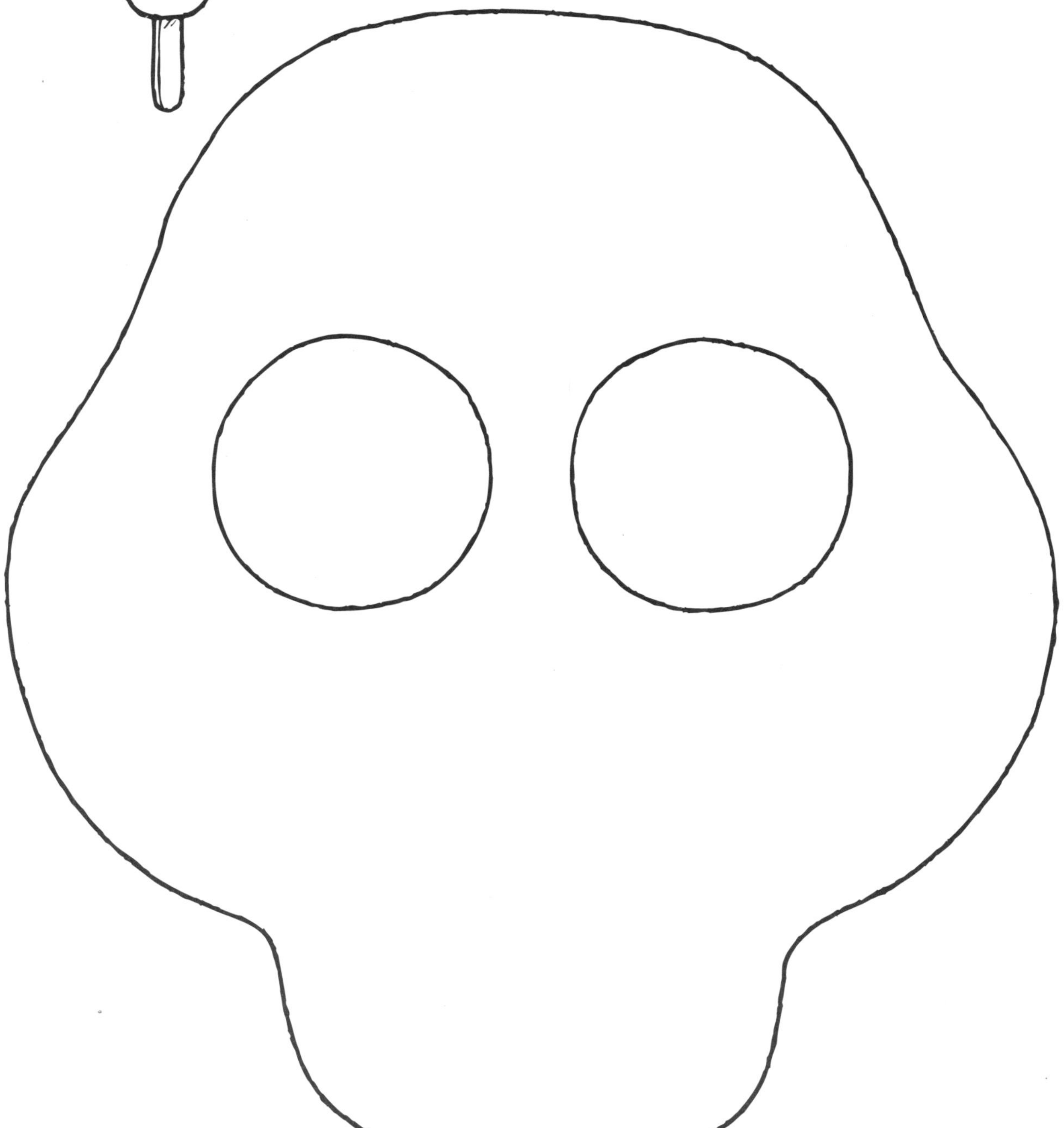

Jump to it!

Learning objective
To listen and respond to instructions.

Group size
Up to four children.

What you need
The photocopiable sheet; an action rhyme; two toy telephones for each pair of children; crayons.

Preparation
Try to find an action rhyme which is new to the children. Copy the photocopiable sheet so that you have one for each child and one for yourself.

What to do
Perform the action rhyme for the children. Encourage them to *listen* to any instructions in the rhyme as well as watching for actions. Now encourage them to join in with the rhyme and the actions.

Individual recording
Put the children in pairs, sitting a little way apart, with a toy telephone each. Begin by showing the children how to speak to each other 'through' the telephone by asking them to do a simple action, such as 'Charlotte, will you please touch your hair?' or 'Harry, can you nod your head?'. Then, encourage the children to take turns giving instructions to each other. Initially, both children should be helped to think of ideas and to carry them out.

Using the photocopiable sheet, let one child give instructions for the action shown in the first illustration. Help as necessary by whispering the instructions. Encourage the second child to try to respond without help. Let the children reverse roles for the next illustration. Continue in this way until they have worked their way through the whole sheet.

Finally, discuss the pictures on the photocopiable sheet and help each child to record the actions that he or she carried out by colouring them in.

Support
Speak directly to each child instead of using a telephone, demonstrating the actions as necessary.

Extension
Develop the activity by asking the children to do two actions in sequence. For example, 'Clap your hands then touch your toes' or 'Sit on the floor and put your hands on your head'.

Assessment
Do the children understand what is required of them? If a child is reluctant to participate, observe how well they listen to instructions in day-to-day activities, and consider whether they are able to hear you, by speaking to them from different directions. How well do they respond to instructions?

Home links
Ask parents to give children clear and simple instructions in the home such as, 'Can you go upstairs and bring me your red jumper please?'.

Jump to it!

Clap your hands

Touch your toes

Touch your head

Sit on the floor

Jump up and down

Walk round a chair

On my holidays

Learning objective
To recount events and experiences to a group.

Group size
Up to five children.

What you need
The photocopiable sheet; display table; a selection of items connected with holidays (for example suitcase, buckets, spades, sand).

Preparation
Make a small holiday display with the collected items. Copy the photocopiable sheet so that you have one for each child and one for yourself.

What you do
Talk about the display with the children, and listen to their responses. Some may react immediately, talking about their holidays. Invite the others to join in. Develop their discussion by asking them in gerneral terms about what they did, for example with their buckets and spades or with their friends. Observe any child not entering into the discussion and try to establish whether they are just reluctant to talk, or whether they didn't have a beach holiday, or even a holiday at all, remembering to be sensitive to individual children's circumstances. You may encourage these children to tell you about a particular day that they might have enjoyed, such as going to a party at a friend's house or visiting the zoo.

Individual recording
Give each child a copy of the photocopiable sheet and encourage them to tell you a more complete version of their holiday, building on the previous discussion. Use the border of the page, showing pictures of a typical seaside holiday, as a prompt to the child's story. Suggest that they draw themselves in the picture. Ask those children who didn't have a beach holiday to tell you about theirs. On the reverse of the sheet, draw a simple border including items more appropriate to their experience (for example camping equipment, items for picnics, funfair rides and so on). They can then draw a picture of themselves on holiday or at home. Afterwards, invite the children to talk in small groups about their holidays, using their pictures to help them. Make observational notes on their sheets.

Support
Some children may prefer to talk about one event, rather than remember the whole holiday. For example, they may just talk about the sandcastle they built, the special toy they bought or where they stayed.

Extension
Encourage the children to talk in greater detail about their holidays, relating as many facts as they can remember.

Assessment
Observe how well the children are able to recount events. Did they maintain a sequence? Did they have difficulty in finding the right words? Were they able to remember the details when retelling to the group?

Home links
Parents can help by encouraging and valuing the child's contribution to family discussions.

On my holidays

Story people

Learning objective
To find out information by asking questions and listening to answers.

Group size
Up to five children.

What you need
The photocopiable sheet; coloured wooden beads; string; a story-book with four main characters; scissors; glue; paper.

Preparation
Thread ten different-coloured wooden beads onto a length of string in a repeating pattern. Adapt the outline figures on the photocopiable sheet to match the characters in the story to be read, by drawing in clothing to distinguish each person. Write the names of the character under their outlines, then copy two photocopiable sheets for each child.

What to do
Give each child a length of string and sufficient beads of the right colour to match the prepared string of beads. Keep your string hidden, but invite the children to try to make one that matches it by asking questions rather than looking at it. Say, 'The first bead is this colour' and hold up an identical bead.

Encourage the children to find out the order of the rest of the beads by asking you questions. For example, they could ask, 'Is it blue?' or they could ask you directly, 'What colour is the next bead?'. As they determine the colour of each bead they should thread it until they have a pattern that matches yours.

Individual task
Read the story and discuss the pictures. Give each child a copy of the photocopiable sheet and help them to identify each character. Look at the book without letting them see the pictures. Ask them to guess which character you are looking at by asking you questions.

Once they have established which one it is, encourage them to find out how to colour in the picture, by asking, 'What colour are the trousers?' (shoes, jumper and so on). Repeat the process with each character. Afterwards the children can cut out and glue the pictures into a zigzag book.

Support
If all the children do not know their colours, hold up a crayon of the right colour as you say, for example, 'Colour the hair brown, like this crayon.'

Extension
Encourage the children to discuss their little books with you afterwards. Ask them to give you information about a character and let you guess which one they are looking at.

Assessment
Did the children listen carefully to instructions? Were the questions they asked relevant to the information they needed?

Home links
Ask parents to hide a selection of small items around the house, and encourage their children to find them by asking questions and following the instructions.

Story people

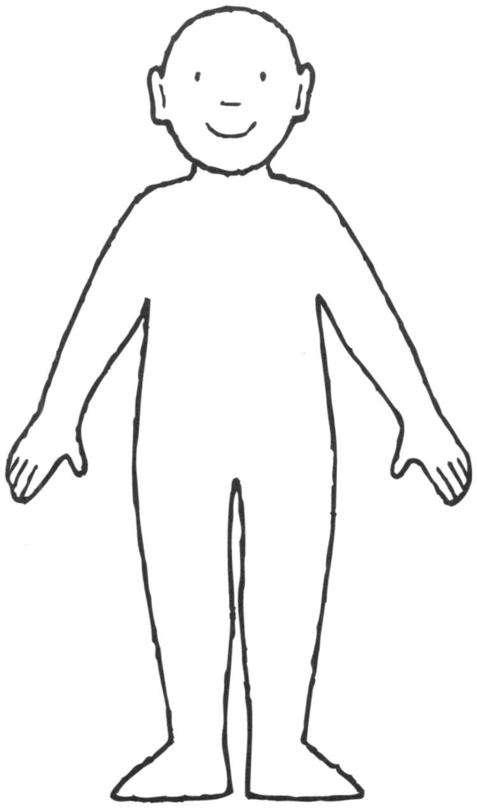

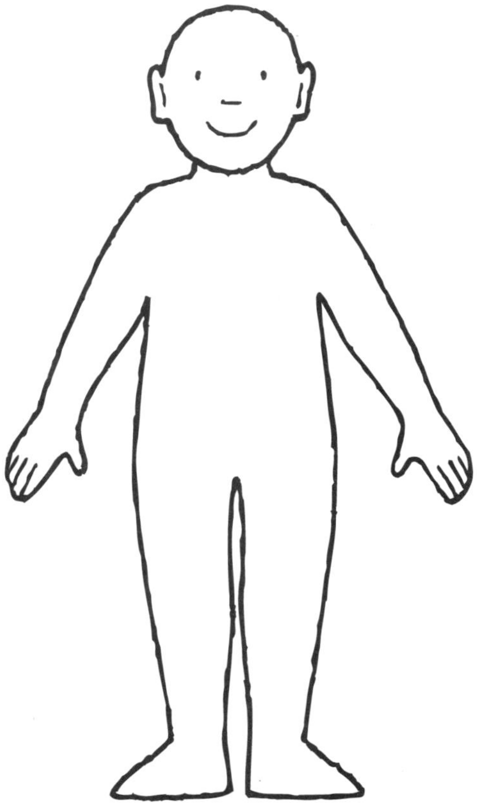

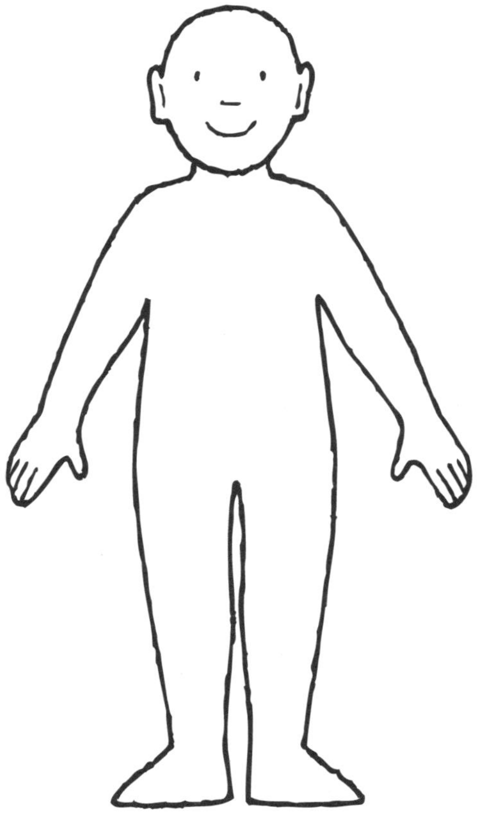

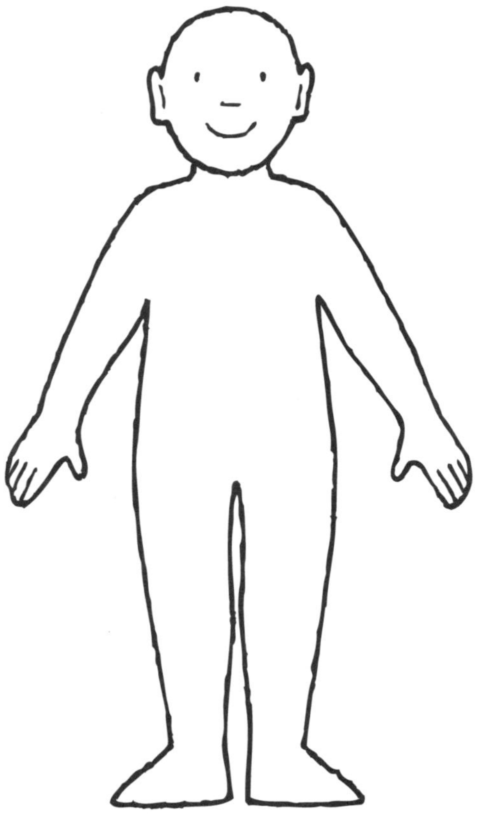

Tell a story

Learning objective

To make up a story and tell it to a group.

Group size

Up to five children.

What you need

The photocopiable sheet; a collection of two or three toys (such as a car, teddy and ball) for yourself; small-world toys for the children; crayons; scissors; glue; plain paper.

Preparation

Prepare a rough outline for a story that you could tell using your toys as props. Copy the photocopiable sheet so that you have two copies for each child.

What to do

Start by letting the children play freely with the small-world toys. Encourage them to tell you about the games that they are playing (which toy is doing what, what happens next and so on).

After ten minutes, sit the children in front of you and say that you would like them to help you make up a story using the selection of toys. Ask them for ideas and begin to tell the story using one of the toys as the central character. Refer to the children from time to time, asking, 'What do you think happened then?'. Keep the story short and simple.

Individual task

Give each child a copy of the photocopiable sheet, keeping the second copies to write comments on. Explain that the pictures are for them to make up a story. Give the children time to look at the pictures and talk about them. Ensure that they know what each one is. Now ask the children to colour in the characters that they want to use in their stories. Help them to cut out those pictures and paste them onto the plain paper as they wish. As this is being done, continue to encourage them to focus on the story and what will happen in the final picture. The stories may change as the children develop new ideas! Gather together again as a group and invite each child to tell the others their story, using their picture as a prompt.

Support

Allow the children to stick their cut-out pictures in any order onto the paper first and then tell their own story.

Extension

Ask the children to draw and colour in a background to the characters in their picture. This may add an extra dimension to their story.

Assessment

Take note of how many pieces of information the children give about the characters and their feelings, the action and setting.

Home links

Ask parents to make up short stories at bedtime occasionally, instead of telling their children a story from a book.

Tell a story

Hey diddle, diddle

Learning objective
To listen and respond to rhymes.

Group size
Up to five children.

What you need
The photocopiable sheet; books of poems and nursery rhymes; crayons; paper.

Preparation
Copy the photocopiable sheet so that you have one for each child and one for yourself.

What to do
Read or tell the children a selection of poems and nursery rhymes, which should *not* include 'Hey Diddle, Diddle'. Talk about the rhymes, and in particular encourage the children to retell the story content. Ask them who is in each rhyme. Show them pictures where possible, and discuss the characters. Return to one of the rhymes and see how many details the children can remember.

Now select one of the more simple nursery rhymes and ask the children to draw a picture about it, encouraging them to talk about their picture as they do so.

Individual recording
Read the nursery rhyme, 'Hey Diddle, Diddle', through once. Give each child a copy of the photocopiable sheet and allow them some time to look at the pictures. Re-read the rhyme, this time asking the children to point to the characters as you mention them. (The sheet contains extra characters who are not in the rhyme, in order to check that children are not guessing haphazardly.)

Afterwards, ask the children to use the crayons to colour in only the pictures of the characters or events in the rhyme. As they complete the activity, ask them questions such as, 'What is the cow doing?' 'What is the dog doing?' 'What is the dish doing?' and so on.

Support
Talk through the pictures on the photocopiable sheet with the children, before reading the rhyme.

Extension
Ask the children to 'read' the rhyme through, using the pictures as an aid.

Assessment
Observe how well the children listened to the selection of rhymes and poems. Did they respond by joining in with any of them? Were they able to recall individual characters? Were they confident and accurate in selecting pictures on the photocopiable sheet? How far could they recite that part of the rhyme relevant to the illustration?

Home links
Ask parents to read poems and rhymes to their children, encouraging them to talk about the characters and what they did.

Hey diddle, diddle

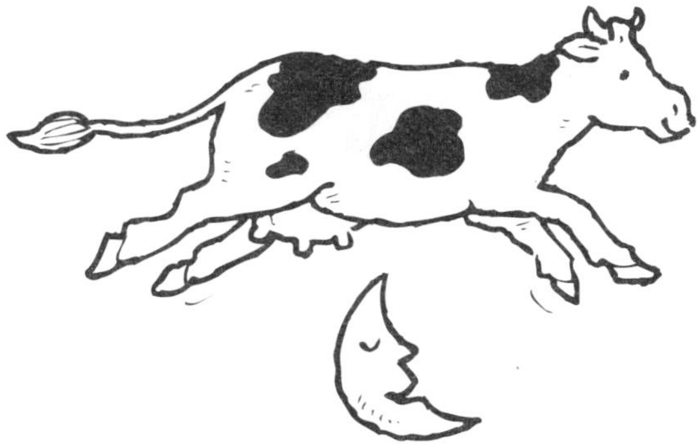

Name ____________________

Skills development chart

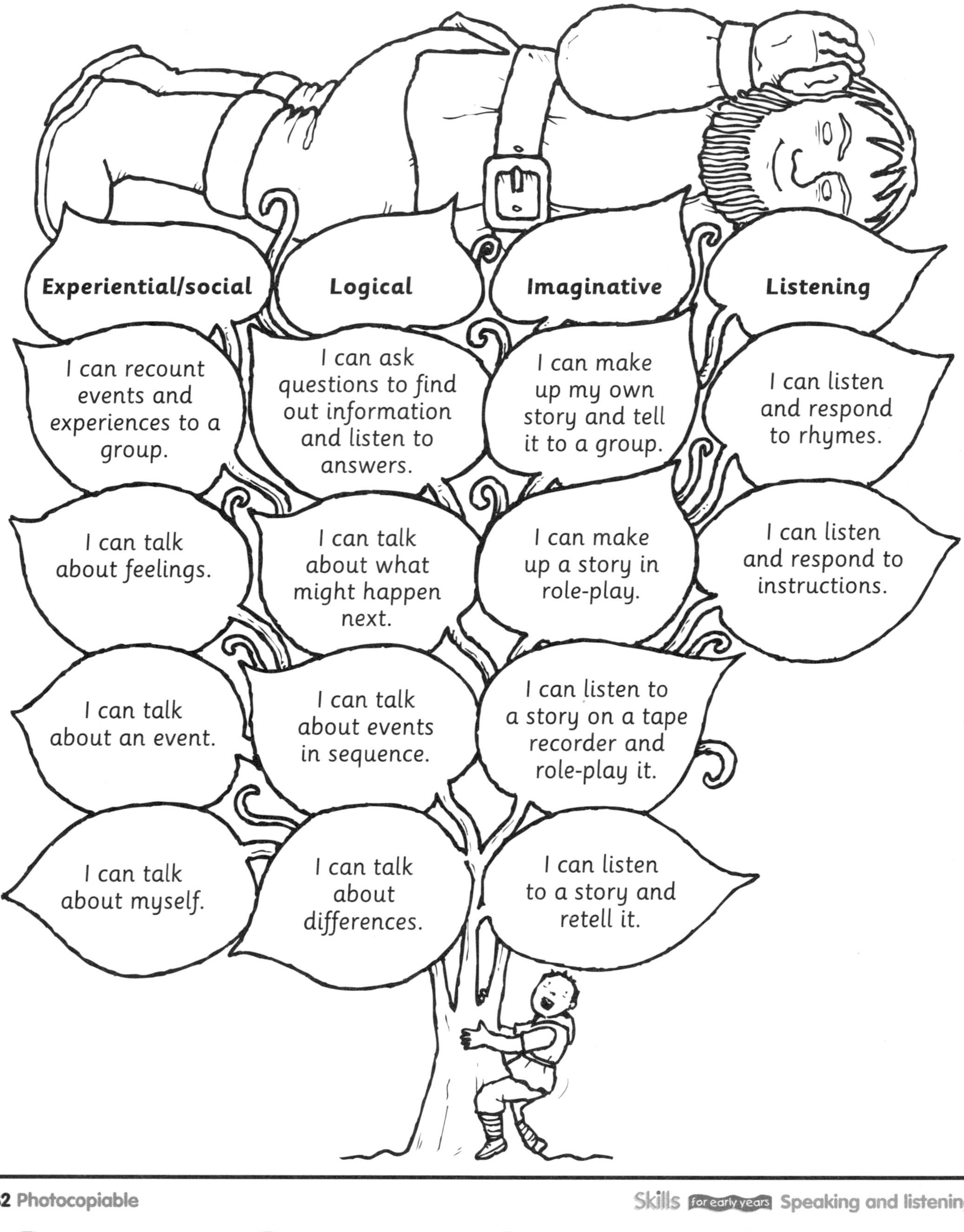